HISTORICAL PERSPECTIVES
In Their Own Words

The Words of HELEN KELLER

Emmett Martin

PowerKiDS press

Published in 2024 by The Rosen Publishing Group, Inc.
2544 Clinton Street, Buffalo, NY 14224

Portions of this work were originally authored by Caroline Kennon and published as *Helen Keller in Her Own Words* (Eyewitness to History). All new material this edition authored by Emmett Martin.

Editor: Therese Shea
Book Design: Michael Flynn

Photo Credits: Cover https://commons.wikimedia.org/wiki/File:Helen_Keller,_no._8_LCCN2009633161.jpg; (series background) merrymuuu/Shutterstock.com; (fact box) Miloje/Shutterstock.com; pp. 5, 9 courtesy of the Library of Congress; p. 7 https://commons.wikimedia.org/wiki/File:Helen_Keller_with_Anne_Sullivan_in_July_1888.jpg; pp. 9 (inset), 11 courtesy of Perkins School for the Blind; p. 10 courtesy of the Boston Public Library; p. 13 https://commons.wikimedia.org/wiki/File:PSM_V63_D081_Helen_keller_and_miss_sullivan.png; p. 15 https://en.wikipedia.org/wiki/Helen_Keller#/media/File:Helen_KellerA.jpg; p. 17 https://commons.wikimedia.org/wiki/File:Helen_Keller15.jpg; p. 18 https://commons.wikimedia.org/wiki/File:Helen_Keller13.jpg; p. 19 courtesy of University Archives, L. Tom Perry Special Collections, Harold B. Lee Library, Brigham Young University; p. 21 (Keller) https://commons.wikimedia.org/wiki/File:Helen_Keller_circa_1920_-_restored.jpg; p. 21 (Bell) https://commons.wikimedia.org/wiki/File:Alexander_Graham_Bell.jpg; p. 23 https://commons.wikimedia.org/wiki/File:Helen_Keller27.jpg; p. 25 AFB Migel Memorial Library Collection, 2009.24; p. 27 Abbie Rowe. White House Photographs. John F. Kennedy Presidential Library and Museum, Boston; p. 28 tristan tan/Shutterstock.com.

Library of Congress Cataloging-in-Publication Data

Names: Martin, Emmett, author. | Kennon, Caroline. Helen Keller in her own words.
Title: The words of Helen Keller / Emmett Martin.
Description: New York : PowerKids Press, [2024] | Series: Historical perspectives: in their own words | "Portions of this work were originally authored by Caroline Kennon and published as Helen Keller in Her Own Words"--Verso. | Includes bibliographical references and index.
Identifiers: LCCN 2022055377 (print) | LCCN 2022055378 (ebook) | ISBN 9781642826982 (library binding) | ISBN 9781642826975 (paperback) | ISBN 9781642826999 (ebook)
Subjects: LCSH: Keller, Helen, 1880-1968. | Deafblind women--United States--Biography--Juvenile literature.
Classification: LCC HV1624.K4 M56 2024 (print) | LCC HV1624.K4 (ebook) | DDC 362.4/1092 [B]--dc23/eng/20230118
LC record available at https://lccn.loc.gov/2022055377
LC ebook record available at https://lccn.loc.gov/2022055378

Manufactured in the United States of America

CONTENTS

THE ILLNESS

In her first **autobiography**, Helen Keller wrote: "The beginning of my life was simple and much like every other little life. I came, I saw, I conquered, as the first baby in the family always does." That little baby would grow to become a champion for people with disabilities around the world. Her life story would inspire millions to **advocate** for others as well.

Keller was born on June 27, 1880, in Tuscumbia, Alabama. When she was around 18 months old, she developed a terrible fever: "The doctor thought I could not live." When the fever finally broke, the family was overjoyed. However, "no one, not even the doctor, knew that I should never see or hear again." Keller never recovered her hearing or sight.

LOOKING BACK

This book uses Helen Keller's own words, from her autobiographies and speeches, to present her remarkable life to readers.

Childhood Interrupted

Helen Keller was a healthy baby. She began walking when she was about one. She had already begun saying her first words when she became sick. After she recovered, she remembered the word "water," but without hearing adults speak, she couldn't improve or build her vocabulary. She felt like she was "at sea in a dense fog." She said, "I ceased making the sound 'wah-wah' only when I learned to spell the word."

Helen Keller said, "I seldom think about my limitations, and they never make me sad."

ANNE'S ARRIVAL

Helen Keller's younger years weren't happy ones. She faced many challenges. Since she couldn't speak, she invented ways of asking for things, but not everyone understood her. She often acted out in violent anger: *"The need of some means of communication became so urgent that . . . outbursts occurred daily."* Keller's parents knew she needed education. However, they *"lived a long way from any school for the blind or the* ***deaf****."* The Kellers asked a teacher to come live with them.

When Helen Keller was six years old, Anne Sullivan arrived at the Keller home. Sullivan had been nearly blind herself, but an operation restored her sight. She had attended the Perkins School for the Blind in Massachusetts. There, she learned how to communicate with a woman who was blind and deaf.

LOOKING BACK

Before Anne Sullivan arrived, Helen Keller had developed her own limited sign language of about 60 signs. Keller could communicate with a young girl named Martha Washington, the daughter of her family's cook.

Discovering Difference

Keller knew she was different from other people. She said, "I had noticed that my mother and my friends did not use signs the way I did . . . Sometimes I would stand between two persons who were conversing and would touch their lips. I could not understand, and was vexed. I moved my lips and **gesticulated** frantically without result. This made me so angry at times that I kicked and screamed until I was exhausted."

Anne Sullivan was 20 years old when she accepted a job with the Kellers. Helen Keller described Sullivan's arrival in 1887 as "the most important day I remember in all my life."

A FAST LEARNER

Anne Sullivan brought Helen Keller a doll. She used her fingers to spell "d-o-l-l" on Keller's palm. She did this with other objects too. At first, Keller didn't understand the link between the touch of Sullivan's fingers and objects, but Sullivan kept trying. Finally, she ran water over Keller's hand and spelled "w-a-t-e-r." Keller made the connection.

Helen Keller wanted to learn more and quickly. She said, *"From the beginning of my education Miss Sullivan made it a practice to speak to me as she would speak to any hearing child; the only difference was that she spelled the sentences into my hand instead of speaking them."*

Just four months after Anne Sullivan arrived, seven-year-old Keller knew how to finger spell hundreds of words and some simple sentences.

LOOKING BACK

Keller could hear the beat of music and enjoyed it. She could also recognize people in her household by the **vibrations** of their footsteps.

On to Writing

Helen Keller began writing a few months after learning to spell words. She placed paper over a board that had the alphabet grooved into it. With patience and practice, she memorized how to move her pencil in order to form the letters. Then she moved on to words, sentences, and finally whole books. She began to write letters to relatives. She sometimes used a ruler to guide her in drawing square block letters.

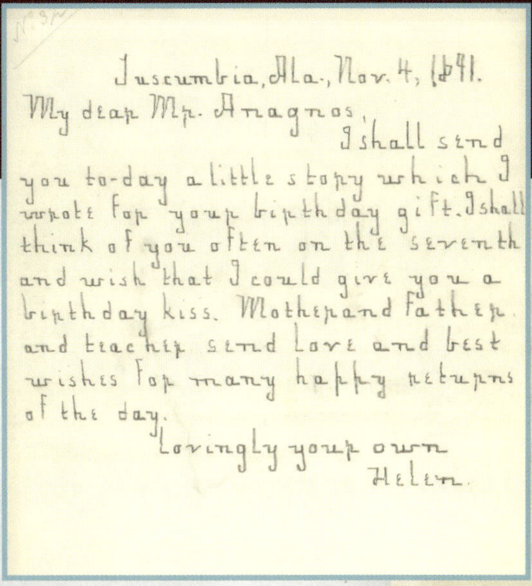

Tuscumbia, Ala., Nov. 4, 1891.

My dear Mr. Anagnos,

I shall send you to-day a little story which I wrote for your birthday gift. I shall think of you often on the seventh and wish that I could give you a birthday kiss. Mother and Father and teacher send love and best wishes for many happy returns of the day.

Lovingly your own

Helen.

Keller later wrote about learning the word for "water": "That living word awakened my soul, gave it light, hope, set it free!"

LEAVING HOME

In 1888, Helen Keller and Anne Sullivan traveled to Massachusetts so Keller could attend Perkins School for the Blind. There, she learned to read using the Braille system of writing, in which letters are represented by raised dots. She also learned to write with a special typewriter. In 1890, Keller began speech classes at Horace Mann School for the Deaf in Boston, Massachusetts. Then, beginning in 1894, she attended Wright-Humason School for the Deaf in New York City to improve her communication skills and to study academic subjects.

Keller decided to go to college: "The thought of going to college took root in my heart and became an earnest desire, which impelled me to enter into competition for a degree with seeing and hearing girls." To prepare, Keller entered the Cambridge School for Young Ladies.

Horace Mann School for the Deaf

The Short Story Incident

In 1891, Helen Keller wrote a story, "The Frost King," for the director of the Perkins School, who then published it. However, people discovered it was much like another published story. Keller had likely read it when she was younger but didn't remember she had. The author of the original work, Margaret Canby, wrote to the upset Keller: "Some day you will write a great story out of your own head, that will be a comfort and help to many."

LOOKING BACK

Sullivan accompanied Keller to the Cambridge School. Keller said, "Each day Miss Sullivan went to the classes with me and spelled into my hand with infinite patience all that the teachers said."

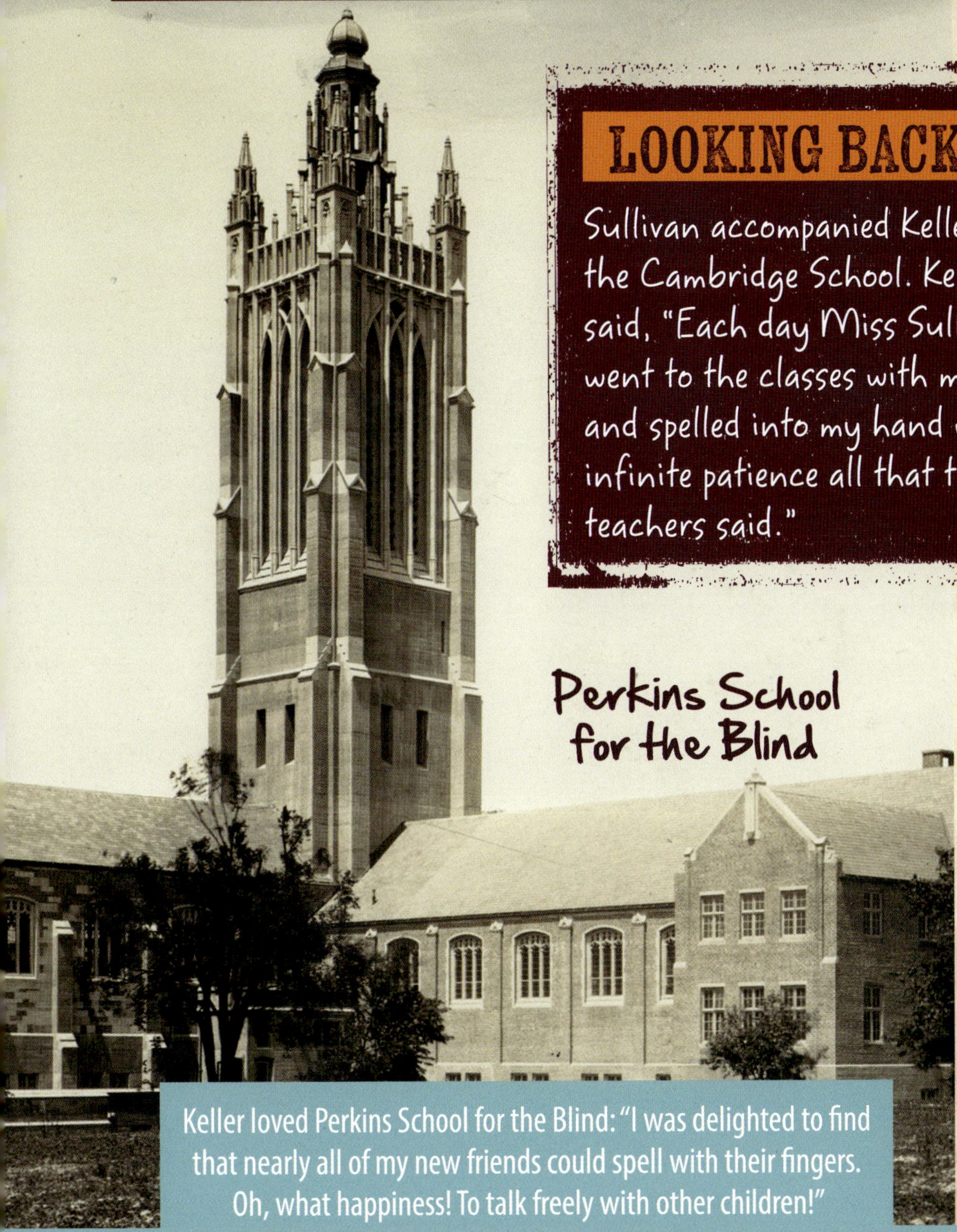

Perkins School for the Blind

Keller loved Perkins School for the Blind: "I was delighted to find that nearly all of my new friends could spell with their fingers. Oh, what happiness! To talk freely with other children!"

RADCLIFFE

In 1900, Helen Keller was accepted into Radcliffe College, then a part of Harvard University. She had only dreamed of this: "*Before me I saw a new world opening in beauty and light, and I felt within me the capacity to know all things. In the wonderland of Mind I should be as free as another.*" Keller believed that education made her the equal of all whose ears could hear and eyes could see.

But college life was difficult. Keller especially struggled with math signs. The school was careful to make sure Sullivan wasn't helping her. Keller was happy, though: "*Knowledge is happiness, because to have knowledge—broad, deep knowledge—is to know true ends from false, and lofty things from low.*" She graduated, with honors, from Radcliffe in 1904.

LOOKING BACK

When Helen Keller graduated from Radcliffe, she became the first person who was deaf and blind to earn a Bachelor of Arts degree.

More About Braille

While Sullivan read some schoolbooks to Keller, others were available in Braille. Braille is a writing system that uses raised dots arranged in patterns so that people can read using their sense of touch. Louis Braille, its inventor, lost his eyesight at the age of three. He created his writing method, still used today, when he was a teenager. By age 10, Keller had learned to read and write Braille. She used a Braille typewriter as well as a standard typewriter.

This 1899 photograph shows Anne Sullivan reading to Helen Keller, by spelling the words of the book in her hand.

THE STORY OF HER LIFE

During her school years, Helen Keller suffered from self-doubt about her abilities and ideas. Sullivan encouraged her to write about her life to boost her **confidence**. In 1903, while still at Radcliffe, Keller published her autobiography, *The Story of My Life*. The book opened: "It is with a kind of fear that I begin to write the history of my life." Keller found it hard to distinguish fact from imagination in her early years. Instead of including every detail, she said, "I shall try to present in a series of sketches only the episodes that seem to me to be the most interesting and important."

Though others were fascinated by her life, Keller didn't always like writing about herself: "I found myself utterly confined to one subject-myself, and it was not long before I exhausted it."

LOOKING BACK

The World I Live In, a book Keller published in 1908, aimed to help others understand what it's like living without sight and hearing. She described how she used her senses of smell and touch as well as her imagination to navigate the world.

Learning to Speak

Helen Keller tried to perfect her speech her whole life: "The impulse to utter audible sounds had always been strong within me." She put her hand on Sullivan's cheek, mouth, and neck and tried to copy the movement and vibration. This is called the Tadoma method, which she learned at Horace Mann School for the Deaf. Yet, without being able to hear her own voice, she couldn't be sure how she sounded.

In 1904, the year this photo was taken, Helen Keller bought her first home, in Wrentham, Massachusetts.

"BOOK-FRIENDS"

Keller had received top grades in English and never stopped reading for pleasure and for education after she left school. She said, "More than at any other time, when I hold a beloved book in my hand my limitations fall from me, my spirit is free."

Keller described books as her friends. In her opinion, books never **discriminate** based on disability or difference. Books, and the stories within them, accepted her without hesitation and allowed her to experience people and places as she never had before: "No barrier of the senses shuts me out from the sweet, gracious discourse of my book-friends."

This love of reading translated into a talent for writing. After her first autobiography, Keller went on to write 11 more books as well as many essays.

LOOKING BACK

Keller owned dogs throughout her life as faithful companions. She once said that if she had vision, "I should like to look into the loyal, trusting eyes of my dogs . . . whose warm, tender, and playful friendships are so comforting to me."

Accused

Sadly, some in Helen Keller's time didn't believe that she could really read or write by herself. Some accused her and Anne Sullivan of trying to trick others about her abilities. They said Sullivan was giving Keller all her ideas. But Keller had famous friends who defended her. These included inventor Alexander Graham Bell and author Mark Twain, who said, "These solemn donkeys breaking a little child's heart with their ignorant . . . rubbish!"

Anne Sullivan challenged Helen Keller at a young age to read classics and not just children's literature.

ON TOUR

Keller began giving lectures in 1913, with the aid of Sullivan. Describing her first talk, Keller wrote, "Terror invaded my flesh, my mind froze, my heart stopped beating." She overcame this feeling, however. Her lectures were popular, and she went on to speak in places around the world for the next 50 years.

With each tour stop, Sullivan spoke about her years with Keller, and then Keller spoke. It was difficult for many people to understand Keller, so Sullivan repeated her words. At the end of the talk, they took questions from the audience. Their tour brought fame and an offer to have Keller's life turned into a black-and-white silent film called *Deliverance*. Produced in 1919, Helen Keller and Anne Sullivan appeared in it.

LOOKING BACK

Helen Keller had her eyes replaced with glass eyes when she was 30 years old. Before this, she was often pictured from the side.

Acting as an Advocate

Helen Keller understood people's interest in her provided her with the opportunity to be an advocate for the rights of those who couldn't hear, see, or speak. She also promoted women's rights, especially the right to vote, which women didn't have until the Nineteenth **Amendment** went into effect in 1920. Interestingly, Keller and Anne Sullivan sometimes disagreed on social issues. However, they agreed in "*our desire of good*" for the world, Keller recalled.

In this photo from 1914, Helen Keller, middle, poses after lecturing at Brigham Young University.

THE AFB

In 1924, Helen Keller became an **ambassador** for the American Foundation for the Blind (AFB), promoting programs that help those with visual loss. "When the public adopts an attitude of understanding and helpfulness, the difficulties of the sightless will no longer be **insurmountable**," she said to an audience. Keller helped raise millions of dollars for the AFB.

In 1925, Keller spoke at a meeting of the Lions Clubs community service organizations. She motivated the creation of their Knights of the Blind: "You who have your sight, your hearing, you who are strong and brave and kind—will you not constitute yourselves Knights of the Blind in my **crusade** against darkness?" This speech led to the Lions Clubs adopting vision loss as a focus for community service.

LOOKING BACK

By 1927, Helen Keller had spoken to about 250,000 people at 249 meetings in 123 cities.

Alexander Graham Bell

Inventor Alexander Graham Bell died in 1922. A teacher of deaf children, he had been an influential part of Helen Keller's life since her parents sought his help in 1886. (This was about 10 years after Bell invented the telephone.) Bell's advice led Keller to meet Anne Sullivan. He helped pay for Keller's education as well. Bell said his work with the deaf was "more pleasing to me than even recognition of my work with the telephone."

Alexander Graham Bell

Helen Keller worked for the AFB for more than 40 years. She worked on projects that gave radios and "talking books" to people with vision loss.

SULLIVAN'S DEATH

In the 1920s, Anne Sullivan began to have health issues and eventually couldn't travel with Helen Keller. A woman named Polly Thomson sometimes took Sullivan's place by Keller's side. On October 20, 1936, Sullivan died.

Sullivan had never taken much credit for Keller's success. She saw herself as a teacher. In a statement before she died, she said: "Thank God I gave of my life that Helen might live."

Shortly after her death, Keller and Polly Thomson traveled to Scotland. On the trip, Keller wrote, "*This is the first voyage Polly and I have had without Teacher, who was the life and the center of our journeyings by land and sea. . . . The anguish which makes me feel cut in two prevents me from writing another word about these life-wrecking changes.*"

LOOKING BACK

Anne Sullivan had married John Albert Macy in 1905, becoming Anne Sullivan Macy, though the couple later separated.

Continuing the Mission

Sullivan had encouraged Keller to travel to Japan where hundreds of thousands of people who were blind or deaf weren't receiving education. In 1937, Keller toured 33 Japanese cities, drawing huge crowds. Newspapers reported her speeches brought audiences to tears. During one, she said, "Love is power. Power is love. Let power and love build an independent and happy life for the physically handicapped. Let the light of sympathy brighten up the darkness of their lives."

Sullivan died while Keller held her hand. Sullivan's ashes were laid to rest in Washington, D.C., at the National Cathedral. She was the first woman honored this way.

ADVOCATE FOR EDUCATION AND EMPLOYMENT

Helen Keller continued to travel the world, speaking out for people with disabilities. At that time, some who were both deaf and blind were sent to live in institutions, away from society. Her advocacy helped establish schools in Africa, Asia, and Latin America for children with vision and hearing loss. She recalled, "I was like [a] ship before my education began, only I was without compass . . . and [I had] no way of knowing how near the harbor was." She wanted others to have the same opportunities she had.

Keller also appealed to employers to hire people who were blind and deaf, and encouraged sports for the blind such as bowling as well as Braille cookbooks. She was for anything that would allow those with disabilities to live a normal life.

LOOKING BACK

Helen Keller supported civil rights for Black Americans. She said, "This great republic of ours is a mockery when citizens in any section are denied the rights which the Constitution guarantees them."

An Advisor for Veterans

Keller spoke on behalf of war veterans who had lost some or all of their vision in World War I, World War II, and the Korean War. She suggested how families should welcome home those who were blinded, and she helped secure funding for veterans' job training and support. She was against war in general but visited many military hospitals around the world. She said that visiting the soldiers who fought selflessly was "the crowning experience" of her life.

Keller meets schoolchildren in Beirut, Lebanon, in 1952.

A LIFETIME OF SERVICE

Keller's companion Polly Thomson died in 1960. *"It will be most lonely for me,"* she wrote to a friend. However, she never felt too sorry for herself: *"Self-pity is our worst enemy and if we yield to it, we can never do anything good in the world."* The same year, Keller had a stroke and decided to stop traveling. Her last public appearance was at a Lions Club International meeting. There, she received an award for her lifetime of service.

In 1964, President Lyndon B. Johnson awarded Keller the Presidential Medal of Freedom, the highest honor awarded to a citizen who isn't a soldier. He described her as "an example of courage to all mankind, . . . illuminating the dark world of the blind and the handicapped." Keller was too ill to accept the award in person.

LOOKING BACK

Keller received honorary degrees from many colleges, including the Universities of Glasgow, Berlin, Delhi, and Johannesburg. She was the first woman to be given one from Harvard University.

On Stage and Screen

In 1957, William Gibson wrote a play called *The Miracle Worker* about the lives of Anne Sullivan and Helen Keller. The title comes from author Mark Twain, who first described Sullivan as a "miracle-worker." Gibson used parts of Keller's *The Story of My Life* to describe key events. The play won several awards and is still performed today. It became a movie of the same name in 1962.

Keller met every U.S. president from Grover Cleveland to Lyndon B. Johnson, a total of 13 presidents.

HER LEGACY

Helen Keller died on June 1, 1968, at her home in Easton, Connecticut. She was 87 years old. Her ashes were placed with Anne Sullivan's and Polly Thomson's at the National Cathedral in Washington, D.C. About 1,200 people attended her funeral, and the choir from the Perkins School for the Blind sang.

Keller's work didn't end with her death. Others carried on her mission, inspired by her life. She never stopped being a champion not only for those who were blind and deaf but for the poor and the powerless. She said, "I do not like the world as it is; so I am trying to make it a little more as I want it." She believed she could change the world, and she did.

LOOKING BACK

In 1988, Keller's family began the Helen Keller Foundation for Research and Education, which has helped fund many successful projects for those with vision loss.

The U.S. Postal Service issued a stamp of Keller and Sullivan in 1980.

Admired, but Criticized Too

Helen Keller wasn't always praised for her views. As a young woman, she embraced **socialism** as a means to correct the inequalities she saw in society. She was also a supporter of **labor unions** during a time when many people disagreed with them. Some people thought these views were anti-American. But Keller was always a supporter of the working class and those in poverty and was interested in correcting injustice.

Timeline of Helen Keller's Life

1880 Helen Keller is born on June 27 in Tuscumbia, Alabama.

1881 Keller develops a fever that leaves her blind and deaf.

1886 Keller and her parents meet with Alexander Graham Bell.

1887 Anne Sullivan arrives in Tuscumbia.

1888 Keller enters Perkins School for the Blind in Massachusetts.

1890 She begins at Horace Mann School for the Deaf in Boston.

1896 Keller enters the Cambridge School for Young Ladies in Massachusetts.

1903 She publishes *The Story of My Life*.

1904 Keller graduates with honors from Radcliffe.

1913 Keller and Sullivan give their first lecture.

1936 Sullivan dies on October 20.

1937 Keller visits Japan.

1946 She begins a world tour of military hospitals and promotes the establishment of schools for those with disabilities.

1964 President Lyndon B. Johnson awards Keller the Presidential Medal of Freedom.

1968 Helen Keller dies on June 1.

GLOSSARY

advocate: One who supports or speaks in favor of something.

ambassador: Someone sent by one group or country to speak for it in different places.

amendment: A change or addition to a constitution.

autobiography: A book written by someone about their life.

confidence: Having the belief that someone or something can succeed.

crusade: An action to promote a cause.

deaf: Unable to hear, partly or completely.

discriminate: To unfairly treat people unequally.

gesticulate: To move arms and hands especially when speaking emotionally.

insurmountable: Describing something that cannot be overcome.

labor union: A group of workers that join together to argue for better benefits.

socialism: A way of organizing a society in which major industries are owned and controlled by the government.

vibration: A rapid movement back and forth.

FOR MORE INFORMATION

Books

Buckley, James. *Helen Keller: Inspiration to Everyone!* San Diego, CA: Portable Press, 2021.

Keppeler, Jill. *Helen Keller and Alexander Graham Bell.* New York, NY: Gareth Stevens Publishing, 2022.

Romero, Libby. *Helen Keller.* New York, NY: DK Publishing, 2019.

Websites

Helen Keller Biography
www.afb.org/about-afb/history/helen-keller/biography-and-chronology/biography
Read Keller's speeches and learn more details about her life.

Helen Keller Timeline
www.perkins.org/resource/helen-keller-timeline/
Find many more facts about Keller's life and legacy, including about the Barbie doll made to honor her in 2021.

INDEX